The No Fuss, No Mess Shape It Up Cookbook

By Nicole Simonin, Health and Fitness Coach

Copyright ©2020 Shape It Up, LLC.

The No Fuss, No Mess, Shape It Up Cookbook

By Nicole Simonin, Health and Fitness Coach

Copyright ©2020 Nicole Simonin

All rights reserved.

This publication is written as a source of information only. The information contained in this book should by no means be considered a substitute for the advice of a medical professional, who should always be consulted before beginning any new diet, exercise, or other health program.

This book has been carefully researched, and all efforts have been made to ensure the accuracy of its information as of the date it is published. The author expressly disclaims responsibility for any adverse effects, damages, or losses arising from the use or application of the information contained herein.

The No Fuss, No Mess Shape It Up Cookbook

By Nicole Simonin

Acknowledgements

I want to thank all my family and friends who have not just supported me in the making of this book but throughout the years.

I want to thank my kids for trying one more recipe that mom made.

I want to thank all the people I have worked with over the years. From starting Shape It Up in 2006 with online training to Mommy and Me bootcamps to Women Bootcamps in the parks and night classes at the local elementary schools to private training and now online coaching.

I have learned so much for every interaction I have had with all the wonderful people that have made Shape It Up what it is today.

From the bottom of my heart...

Thank You!

Some extra videos that you might find helpful:

Go to YouTube and search

"Nicole Simonin"

Under my playlists go to

"What and How To Eat"

There are helpful videos for you!

Lose the
weight for the
last time.

ShapeItUpFitness.com

Table of Contents

Introduction

I want to tell you a secret...I am not a chef. I barely even consider myself a cook. But I do eat, and I enjoy tasty foods...and if I can attempt to make food healthy AND tasty, I am all in!

Another secret I want to share with you is...I am lazy when it comes to the kitchen.

I hate doing dishes and considering I haven't used a dishwashing machine since 2003 (not by choice...a story for another day) ... I wash everything by hand. If I can make my meals in one pot or pan, I am all for it!

Another secret...I don't like to hunt for rare foods. I would love to go to the natural food markets every week, but I live out in the country and I would have to drive 30-45 minutes to get to one. Making the grocery trip a good 3-4 hours out of my day. I don't have time for that, and I am sure if you picked up this book you don't either. I would rather use that time with my family or serving clients. So, I stick to the local grocery stores and local farmer's markets (when in season).

Last little secret...I hate to food log. Yes, I am a personal trainer and a health coach, but I hate measuring, logging and calculating everything I eat. I teach my clients how to eat without food logging. Occasionally, I will have a client food log just so they have an idea of what is actually going on but I want my clients to enjoy eating without all the extra food drama. This is why the *"The No Fuss, No Mess Shape It Up Cookbook"* was made. Last secret...it was really created out of my selfish need to NEVER FOOD LOG AGAIN!

If you are looking to lose weight or inches, decrease body fat, or just feel more comfortable in your own skin, without fuss, with minimal mess... then this cookbook is for you!

I don't know about you but if I see a recipe that has a huge list of ingredients and 20 steps...my eyes start to glaze over and I will want to grab something less healthy that I think is "easy". This is why all the Shape It Up recipes are neither complicated nor complex. Just simple recipes that will help you reveal the leaner, healthier version of you that is just waiting to come out.

Bon appetite!

Nicole Simonin

ShapeItUpFitness.com

Pineapple Strawberry Pudding Cake

ShapeItUpFitness.com

Shape It Up!

Ginger Shrimp

ShapeItUpFitness.com

Shape It Up!

Banana Strawberry Roll Up

ShapeItUpFitness.com

Shape It Up!

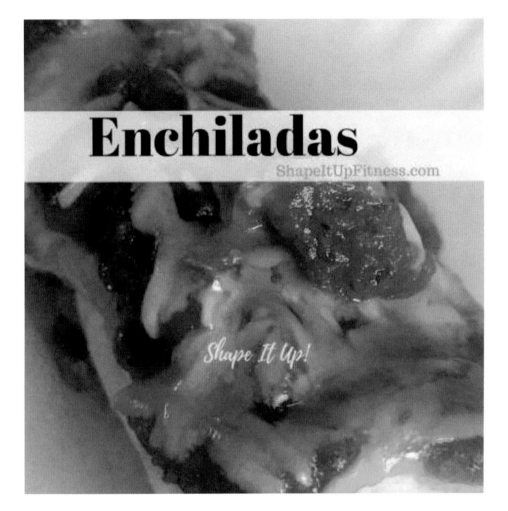

Enchiladas

ShapeItUpFitness.com

Shape It Up!

Thanksgiving Loaf

ShapeItUpFitness.com

Shape It Up!

How To Use This Cookbook

If you want to lose weight or body fat select 3-4 meals per days. Healthy scale weight loss is 1-2 pounds per week. There is a difference between losing scale weight and body fat. This is where having a coach custom design a program specifically for your goals is recommended. (You can learn more about how to do this at ShapeItUpFitness.com).

If you are losing more than 2 pounds per week, you are no longer losing body fat you are losing precious muscle and water.

Patience is key here.

 Losing the weight slow and steady will help you keep it off for life.

The only exception to that rule is if you are brand new to this style of eating and you have over 50 pounds to lose. So, you may have a larger initial drop in weight during the first week or two. If you continue after the second week to lose more than 2 pounds per week, you need to increase your meals. Just add in an additional meal and see what happens. (Again, this is where a health coach would come in handy).

Want some meal plan ideas for the week?

Go here and download your free Shape It Up Meal Plans to use with this cookbook!
https://www.shapeitupfitness.com/meals

Grab Your Bonus!

ShapeItUpFitness.com/meals

Serving Sizes

The recipes listed are mainly for one serving. It will be noted if the serving size is different. I focus on what I like to call "power cooking". This is where I am able to save time in the kitchen. An example of power cooking is instead of making one pound of chicken I will make four pounds of chicken in one shot (hence less pans to clean). More information on power cooking in the upcoming pages. So, most of these recipes are grab and reheat types of meals. If you want to make a meal for six people simple multiple the single serving size by six.

Power Cooking

Planning is the key to the Shape It Up Meals. Make your individual food in advance so it's easy to grab and go!

What is power cooking?

Power cooking is when you make a bunch of food in one shot.

Don't get nervous!

I want this to be simple for you. This is just a template for power cooking. Get good at this version and then you can adapt it to your particular lifestyle once you get the hang of it.

Instead of cooking four ounces of chicken each night, cook 16 ounces of chicken. Now, you have four 4-ounce portions of chicken to use in future meals. Once the chicken is cooked you can either place it in the refrigerator (labeled and dated) or bag it, tag it and freeze it.

If you do this 1-2 times per week with different foods, you will be stocked. You will be able to grab any combination of food and assemble them quickly. Talk about a time saver during the week! Plus, if you have picky eaters in your house, they can grab different foods that are already cooked and pre-portioned, put them on a plate and heat them up. Everyone can eat what they want. Win- win!

Example Of How I Power Cook

Just after coming back from the grocery store, I have purchased the following items:

3lbs of Ground Turkey

10-12 Yams or Sweet Potatoes

I start with the yams. Clean them and place them on a lightly sprayed baking sheet. Bake the yams in oven for about one hour at 350 degrees F. While they are cooking, I divide the ground turkey. I separate each pound of turkey into three separate bowls.

The first bowl, I add ingredients to make into meatballs. The second bowl of turkey, I mix the ingredient to make turkey burgers. The third bowl, the turkey gets seasoned with spices and thrown into a pan to cook.

While the third portion of turkey is now cooking on the stove, I roll the meatballs and I can either cook them now or freeze them. The turkey burgers I make into patties and lay on wax paper on a rack so they can be frozen. I will keep an eye on the turkey in the skillet (this turkey will just get put into a container that will stay in the fridge or I can freeze it into portions). The raw meatballs and burgers will be portioned out, bagged and labeled then sent to the freezer.

After the yams are cooked and cooled, remove the skin, portion them, bag it, tag it and freeze it or place them in a large container and store in the refrigerator for scooping out on the go. All of this will take under an hour and you have just made at least twelve different meals you can grab, heat and go. Plus, you can make each meal unique by changing out condiments, sauces and different foods.

You can do this with <u>any</u> combination of ingredients.

Another option is if you are making a meal, make four times as much as you would normally. Portion and bag the extra meals. Just make sure that you know you actually enjoy the meal. There is nothing worse than making a big batch of food and then not wanting to eat it.

Make sure you label the food: what it is, date and portion size (ounces or grams if you decide to be more precise with weighing).

Power Cooking For The Week Example

This an example of how to start power cooking. Keep in mind, you will fell like you are cooking more initially but I promise after a few batches you will have more food and less cooking time in the kitchen.

Saturday

Cook 15 large yams and 4 lbs. of chicken

Sunday

Cook a week's worth of oatmeal and 4 lbs. of ground turkey (you will see in the future page how this will make burgers, meatballs and ground turkey for chili).

Monday

2-3 boxes of Pasta or rice

Tuesday & Wednesday – NOTHING

Thursday

Cook 2 lbs. of spaghetti squash and shrimp

Friday – Nothing (order out or go out to eat)

Then pick something new to make for the following week. Once you do this rotating foods (making then freezing), you will have a stockpile of foods to grab. This comes in handy if you should get sick or life gets busy, you will always have no fuss foods ready (a.k.a. no excuses to staying on your weight loss goals).

Two Processes

I use two ways to make my meals no fuss to make:

Bag 'em and Tag 'em Process

Scoop And Go Process (SAG)

Bag 'em and Tag 'em Process

Bag and freeze foods for easy grab and go options.

Use for either cooked or raw food. Pre-portion your foods and put them in a snack or sandwich size resealable plastic bag. Label each of the little bags whatever food item is inside for example "4 oz BBQ Chicken". Then place all the little bags into a large gallon size plastic freezer bag. Label the freezer bag and place flat in your freezer.

*(It's really important that you lay the bags flat. This way the bag will take up less space and the food will not freeze into a solid block making defrosting a nightmare).

Scoop And Go Process (SAG)

If I know I will be eating a particular food quite often throughout the week, I will just put the food item in the fridge. This is so I don't have to thaw or defrost anything. An example would be… I eat a ton of yams throughout the week, so after I cook my yams I will place them in a large container in my fridge so I can just scoop and go. If it is getting to be 4-5 days and there is still a good deal of food (let's say yams) left in the fridge container, I will then freeze (using the Bag 'em and Tag 'em process) the rest so I am not wasting any food.

Date Your Food

In either the Bag 'em and Tag 'em or the Scoop And Go processes, I always make sure there is a date on the containers or bags. This makes cleaning out the fridge and freezer super simple and lets you know what needs to be eating as soon as possible. For the frigerated containers, I will use either plastic or glass containers and I will use a dry erase marker to label and date the food. For the bags, I will use a permanent marker for labeling and dating.

₄ying

These are the items I like to buy in bulk:

Chicken, Turkey, beef and pork (all varieties of cuts or ground)

Frozen seafood: shrimp, scallops, tuna steak, salmon steak

Frozen vegetables: broccoli, green beans

I buy raw organic spinach, wash it then freeze it

Frozen fruits (for smoothies)

Unsweetened Almond Milk

Potatoes: sweet, yams, russet and red

Old Fashioned Oatmeal

Coconut oil

What To Power Cook

The following list are easier when you power cook them ahead of time:

- Oatmeal
- Eggs (omelets, egg muffins, hard boiled eggs)
- Beef, Pork, Chicken, Steak and Turkey (whether it is ground, breast, drumstick, etc.)
- Soups
- Vegetables:
    - Any types of vegetables
    - Get frozen vegetables when not in season or but in season and freeze.
- Potatoes: Yams, Sweet, and White Potatoes
- Rice, couscous, quinoa, pilaf *if using boxed versions, you can use half the packet of seasoning to cut down on sodium and I suggest using half the recommended oil or butter based on the individual box's directions.
- Pasta

You really could power cook anything. The skies the limit. Most foods freeze well. Any that aren't mentioned in this book might be trial and error for you to experiment with.

TIP: the only foods I have found that aren't fabulous after freezing are eggs. If you make the omelets and freeze them this is my best tip to avoid soggy eggs. Place them in the microwave to reheat on 50% power. Once out take a paper towel or napkin and soak up any water then eat them. You can also reheat in a pan and let the water dissipate.

Basic Instructions For Power Cooking

Here are some basic cooking directions

Power Cooking Vegetables

I like to get vegetables that are in season but if not available my go-to is frozen vegetables. For fresh vegetables, I will cut them, cook them (steam or sauté with spray olive or coconut oil) then I bag and freeze them or leave them in the fridge for the week. Frozen vegetables can be microwaved and used throughout the week as needed.

Side Note: I use broccoli a lot with these recipes, but you can substitute any fibrous vegetable in place of it (cauliflower, zucchini, etc.)

Power Cooking Eggs

How to Hard Boil Eggs – *(Don't laugh. I remember having to call my mom on how to boil eggs).*

Place eggs gently in pot and cover with cold water just so it just covers the eggs completely.

Place pot on stove top without lid.

Cook on high until the water boils.

Place lid on pot, turn heat off and remove pan from hot burner.

Set a timer for 20 minutes and let eggs sit in pot.

After 20 minutes, take out eggs and place them in a large bowl that is filled with ice and cold water.

Leave eggs in ice bath for about 10-15 minutes.

Take them out and peel them (they are easier to peel if you do this right after the ice bath).

Place the de-shelled eggs in a container.

These eggs will last about one week in the fridge.

To make them last longer, everyday rinse them with cold water in the container and drain water.

Replace back into fridge.

Power Cooking Spaghetti Squash

I find that the 2-3 lbs. squash is easiest to cook.

Rinse the squash off.

With a knife, carefully poke about 10 slits into the squash all over.

Place squash in a large microwave safe bowl.

Place in microwave and cook on HIGH for about 3-5 minutes depending on the size of the squash.

Check on the squash by pushing on the flesh to see if it gives. If it is still pretty firm continue to cook it on HIGH for an additional 1-2 minutes until it is cooked. You can repeat this "1-2 minutes on HIGH" until cooked.

IMPORTANT: Do NOT cook it on HIGH for 10 minutes straight. You do not want the squash to explode in the microwave, I speak from firsthand experience….it is very messy.

Once squash is cooked, place it on counter to cool for about 10-15 minutes. If you can touch it without burning your fingers it is ready to cut.

Carefully, cut the ends of the squash off.

Place squash up on its end and cut it lengthwise in half.

Once cut, scoop out the seeds and discard them.

Taking a fork, scrape out the flesh of the squash (it will look like strings).

Continue to scrape until you get to the shell of the squash.

 Discard seeds and shell.

Store squash in container in fridge for about 3-4 days (SAG) or use the Bag 'em and Tag 'em Process.

Portion suggestions: ¾ cup -1 cup or 150-200 grams

Power Cooking Spuds (Yams, Sweet or White Potatoes)

Set oven to 350 degrees F.

Scrub your spuds under cold water and brush with a vegetable brush getting all the loose dirt off. Remove any eyes or roots.

Spray a baking pan with cooking spray.

Place spuds on baking tray.

Place in oven.

Bake for 60 minutes at 350 degrees F.

Check on them. If they are easy to squish, then they are done.

Take them out of oven.

Let them cool.

Once they are cool to the touch, peel skin off or leave the skin on if you enjoy eating the skin.

Use the Bag 'em and Tag 'em Process or SAG.

Portion suggestions: ¾ cup -1 cup or 150-200 grams

Cooking Ground Meats

If you have frozen your meats when they are raw, make sure they are completely thawed before cooking. Personally, I find the meat tastes better when you let them defrost naturally in the fridge as opposed to defrosting them in the microwave. The meat tends to come out more tender and moist when thawing naturally whereas microwave defrosting tends to dry the meat out or starts to cook it unevenly.

Heat a large pan on the stove and spray with olive oil. Place raw meat into pan and spread it out with a fork. I add spices to the meat or make it plain and add spices as you eat it. If you add spice as you eat the meat you are open to more diversity in your meals.

Once the meat starts to brown on the bottom, flip it over and start stirring and "chopping" the meat into small bits until it is JUST cooked. If you over cook the meat, when you reheat it the meat will be rubbery and dry.

Portion suggestions: 3-4 ounces

TIP: Cook meats to medium temperature. This helps when you reheat the meat. If the meat is a little under done when you power cook, it will be medium-well to well when you go to reheat it later.

Power Cooking Oatmeal and other "cooked" cereals

I like to make six servings of oatmeal for the week, so I will add up the servings size on the oatmeal label and multiple the servings size by six. For instance, one serving of my oatmeal is 30 grams. Multiply by six so I will pour 180 grams into the pot.

Why 6 servings? Glad you asked!

When the oatmeal is cooked, I pour it into a glass 8x8 dish so it will cool and place in refrigerator. Once it has set, it's much easier to cut it into 6 squares than it is into 5 or 7 squares. You can absolutely pick whatever total servings you want. Six works for me because as you will read below, I put the six servings in smaller containers and grab and go throughout the week. (Day 7, I usually make something different like pancakes or French toast).

Place total servings of old-fashioned oats in a large pot and add water until it covers the oats.

Wait until the oats start to boil.

Turn the heat down.

 Let simmer.

While it is at a simmer (really, slow boil), I will slowly add about 2 oz of water (a total of about 16 oz of water) as it is boiling. This will get the oatmeal super creamy.

Once it is cooked, I pour into a glass 8x8 dish, cover with aluminum foil.

Place in fridge and let it cool overnight.

In the morning, I will cut the oatmeal into 6 servings and scoop into smaller containers.

Must-Haves For The Kitchen

Scale to measure your portions (you can absolutely eyeball this but portioning it out is helpful when using the recipes).

Salad Spinner

Double Blade Salad Scissors

Single Blade Kitchen Scissors

Measuring Cups and Spoons

Blender for Smoothies OR Shaker Cup for quick on the go shakes

Containers: glass and/or plastic

Plastic storage bags: Gallon size, Quart size and Snack size

Gallon Freezer Bags

A Note On Sugar and Sugar Substitutes

When I list "low-sugar" in recipes, I am not talking about products that have artificial sweeteners. Most of the products I use have natural sugar but very low content. Make sure you read your food labels.

Aim to get real ingredients and as little processed ingredients as possible.

Avoid like the plague:

> Sucralose and artificial sweeteners

Side Note: To clarify, sucrose is table sugar and sucralose (with an "L") is an artificial sweetener most commonly known as Splenda.

> Stevia (processed)

> BHT, QBHT and other preservatives

> High Fructose Corn Syrup (HFCS)

> Any ingredient you cannot pronounce

There are going to be times when you will eat something from the list above, as long as it's once in a blue moon all should be good.

Sugars that are recommended:

> Honey

> Natural Stevia

> Table sugar (sucrose)

Just use the sugar in moderation. You want to aim to keep blood sugar stable with small fluctuations. Really the less sugar the better.

BREAKFAST

Garden Omelet

6 egg whites

¼ cup of raw spinach

½ Roma tomato

¼ cup mushrooms

1/8 cup cheddar cheese

Pour eggs and vegetables into sprayed heated pan.

When eggs start to solidify, flip omelet over and cook the other side.

Add cheese.

Fold egg over to melt cheese.

Serves 1

Breakfast Skillet Omelet

2 slices turkey bacon

½ cup potato (shredded)

1 cup spinach

4 egg whites

   1/8 cup cheddar cheese

   Salt and pepper to taste

   Place bacon on pan and cook according to package instructions.

   Remove from pan and keep warm.

   Add potato to hot pan.

   Sprinkle with salt and pepper.

   Continue to stir on medium-high heat.

   Once potatoes are cooked, add spinach and pour in eggs.
   Stir to cook.
   Top with cheese.
   Cover pan with lid and lower heat until cheese is melted.

   Serves 1

Omelet Roll Up

1 flour tortilla (low carb option)

4 egg whites

¼ sup salsa

1/8 cup avocado (mashed)

1/8 cup Mexican blend cheese

Spray pan with cooking spray.

Heat pan on medium.

Add eggs and stir until cooked.

Add salsa and cheese until heated.

Place tortilla on plate.

Place omelet on tortilla.

Top with avocado.

Serves 1

English Breakfast Pizza

1 English muffin

4 egg whites

¼ cup spaghetti sauce

1/8 cup mozzarella cheese (shredded)

Fresh basil to taste (chopped)

Cook egg whites in small sprayed pan.

Toast English muffing in toaster.

Once eggs are cooked (while still in pan) gently "cut" (with spatula) the egg into four pieces.

Top evenly with spaghetti sauce and cheese.

When cheese is melted add basil.

    Place toasted English muffins on plate.
    Top each muffin side with a half of egg.

Serves 1

Bacon Cheddar Omelet

4 egg whites

3 slices Canadian bacon (chopped)

1/8 cup sharp cheddar cheese

Pour eggs into a sprayed pan.

When first side sets, flip over.

In same pan (just push egg to side), add bacon.

Stir bacon.

When warm, place bacon on egg and top with cheese.

Serves 1

Banana Strawberry Roll Up

¼ cup prepackaged protein pancake mix

¾ cup egg whites

1/8 cup banana (chopped)

1/8 cup strawberries (chopped)

1/8 cup pure maple syrup

Whisk pancake mix and eggs together.

Pour into sprayed hot pan.

Heat on low-medium heat.

Flip when first side light golden brown.

Add banana, strawberries and syrup.

Fold up and serves.

TIP: I like to use a smaller pan – makes the pancake fluffier. If you want a more crepe texture, use a bigger pan. Note that thinner pancake may break easier.

Serves 1

Chicken Omelet

¾ cup egg whites

1-2 oz chicken (pulled apart and cooked)

2 cups spinach

1/8 cup feta cheese (low-fat)

Pour eggs into a hot sprayed pan.

When eggs start to set, flip to cook other side.

In same pan, (I just push the egg off to the side of pan), add the chicken to reheat.

Once chicken ins warm, place on egg.

Place spinach on eggs and put lid on the pan to wilt the spinach.

As spinach cooks down, leave lid "cracked" on pan so some air escape and the omelet does not get watery.

When spinach is wilted add feta cheese.

Serves 1

PB & J Overnight Oats

1 scoop protein powder

1 Tbsp peanut butter powder

4 ½ oz unsweetened vanilla almond milk

1/8 cup old fashioned oats

1 Tbsp strawberry fruit spread

Using a small mason jar, whisk protein powder, peanut butter powder and milk together.

Add rest of ingredients and stir.

Place in refrigerator.

Next morning take out and stir.

Serves 1

Apple Roll Up

1 cup egg whites

1/8 cup old fashioned oats

1 tsp vanilla extract

1 apple (about ½ cup) chopped

Cinnamon to taste

Drizzle of pure maple syrup

Place oats in a blender and blend until become powder.

Add eggs, oats and extract in blender and blend.

Spray pan with cooking spray.

Add egg mix to pan.

When eggs start to set, flip to cook other side.

Remove from pan and keep warm.

Place chopped apples in pan and sprinkle cinnamon on them.

If apples start to stick, just add a little bit of water to pan.

Stir and sauté.

Cook until tender.

Add back in eggs to reheat.

Place apples on top of eggs.

Drizzle syrup on top and fold eggs over.

Serves 1

Simple Veg N' Eggs

¾ cup egg whites

¾ cup shredded potatoes

¼ cup broccoli (cooked)

Pour eggs into sprayed pan.

Flip when first side starts to set.

Remove from pan and keep warm.

In same pan, re-spray pan and add potatoes.

Add slat and pepper to taste.

Sauté until slightly brown and crispy.

Add broccoli to pan to reheat.

Serves 1

Garden Omelet 2

½ cup egg whites

1 whole egg

½ cup mushrooms (cooked)

1 Roma tomato (chopped)

¼ onions (chopped or sliced)

½ cup shredded potato

Using medium size pan, spray with cooking spray.

Heat on medium-high heat.

Add onions, mushrooms and tomato.

Stir until cooked.

Remove veggies and keep them warm.

Add potatoes and cook until crispy.

Remove potatoes and keep them warm.

Lower heat to medium-low, respray pan if needed.

In small bowl, crack egg and mix in egg whites, whisk until blended.

Place veggies back into pan and reheat.

Pour eggs into pan.

Cook until eggs are firm.

Plate potatoes and place omelet on top.

Serves 1

Eggs and Toast

2 whole eggs

1 slice of Ezekiel bread or 1 English muffin

½ Tbsp butter

1 tsp fruit spread

Cook eggs how you like (scrambled, over easy, poached, etc.).

Toast bread.

Top with butter and fruit spread.

Serves 1

Flipped French Toast

1 Tbsp butter (softened)

1 tsp sugar

Cinnamon to taste

1 cup egg whites

2 oz orange juice

1 oz unsweetened vanilla almond milk

½ tsp vanilla extract

1 oz pure maple syrup

4 slices cinnamon raisin bread

Heat oven to 400F

In an 8x8 baking dish, spread softened butter evenly.

Sprinkle ½ tsp sugar over butter.

In separate bowl, whisk eggs, orange juice, extract and syrup together.

Dip one slice of bread into egg mixture then coat the other side of bread with egg mix.

Lay slice of bread in the baking dish.

Repeat this will all the slices of bread.

Pour rest of egg mixture over the bread.

Sprinkle rest of cinnamon and sugar on top.

Bake 20-25 minutes or until set.

Let it cook for 2 minutes then flip it out onto a serving plate.

Serves 2

Raisin Ricotta Toast

½ cup ricotta cheese, fat free

1 tsp sugar

1 tsp vanilla extract

Cinnamon to taste

2 slices of cinnamon raisin bread

Set oven to broil.

Mix all the ingredients except the bread.

Place bread on ungreased shallow baking pan.

Top bread with ricotta mixture.

Broil for 2-3 minutes or until hot.

Serves 1

Quick Quiche

2 cups egg whites

4 oz unsweetened plain almond milk

Pepper to taste

Dash of nutmeg

1 cup spinach (chopped)

3 oz low-fat Feta cheese

10 slices of Canadian bacon (chopped)

Preheat oven to 350 F

Spray an 8x8 baking dish with cooking spray.

Whisk eggs, milk and spices in large bowl.

Mix in spinach and feta.

Layer Canadian bacon on bottom of baking dish.

Pour egg mixture over bacon.

Bake for 35-40 minutes.

Let it cool for 5 minutes before serving.

Serves 4

Breakfast Date Bars

Crust

Dry Ingredients

1 ½ cup old fashioned oats, blended

½ cup brown sugar

½ cup coconut sugar

1 cup flour

½ tsp baking soda

¼ tsp salt

Wet Ingredients

1/3 cup unsweetened applesauce

½ cup egg whites

Filling

1 cup dates, pitted and chopped

¾ cup water

½ Tbsp orange juice

Preheat oven to 350 F

Crust:

Mix all dry ingredient in large bowl.

Mix all wet ingredients in separate smaller bowl.

Set aside both bowls.

Making filling:

Place dates, water and orange juice in small saucepan.

Bring to a boil while stirring constantly.

Once at a boil lower to a simmer.

Continue to simmer for about 5 minutes stirring the whole time.

Set aside to cool.

While date mix is cooling, spray cooking spray on an 8x8 pan.

Mix the dry and wet ingredients together until it becomes a smooth consistency to make the crust.

Take half of the crust mix and layer the pan.

Spread the date mixture on top.

Finish off with the rest of the crust mixture.

Serves 8

Easy Peasy Eggs

4 egg whites

½ cup cooked potato

1 cup cooked broccoli

1 Tbsp ketchup

Spray pan and heat on medium heat.

Add eggs.

After eggs firm up, flip to cook on other side.

Add potato and broccoli to pan to reheat.

Slide all onto plate.
Add ketchup.

Serves 1

Coconut Eggs and Oats

¼ tsp coconut oil

1 egg (whole)

4 egg whites

1/3 cup dry oatmeal (or oat bran)

1 tsp honey

1 tsp unsweetened coffee creamer

Cinnamon and nutmeg to taste

Place oil in pan and let melt.

When pan is hot pour eggs into pan.

Once eggs firm up, flip over to cook the other side.

Make oats according to brand's directions (omitting sale).

Once oats are cooked, add honey, creamer, cinnamon and nutmeg.

Serves 1

Mexican Omelet

¾ cup egg whites

½ cup potatoes (shredded or thinly sliced)

¼ cup salsa

1/8 cup avocado

Taco spices to taste

Spray medium sized pan with cooking spray over medium-high heat.

Cook potato until crispy.

Remove potatoes and keep warm.

Lower heat to medium- low.

Re-spray pan if needed, add eggs and cook.

Add salsa and taco seasoning.

Plate with potatoes then eggs and top with avocado.

Serves 1

Yam Omelet

6 egg whites

2 slices Canadian Bacon

½ cup cooked yam

1/8 cup white sharp cheddar cheese

Spray medium pan with cooking spray.

Heat on medium.

Add eggs to hot pan.

When eggs firm up, flip over to cook other side.

Fold omelet in half and slide cooked egg to one side of pan.

Add the Canadian bacon and yams to the open side of pan to reheat.

Once bacon and yams are warm, unfold omelet and place bacon, yam and cheese in center of eggs.

Fold over omelet to melt the cheese.

Serves 1

Nutty Oatmeal

6 egg whites

¾ cup cooked oatmeal

Cinnamon and nutmeg to taste

1 tsp honey

5 almonds (chopped)

Using a medium size pan, spray with cooking oil.

Place over medium heat.

Add eggs.

Cook until eggs firm up then flip them over until cooked.

Serve on plate.

In separate pot, cook the oatmeal according to directions on package or use my power cooking method.

Once cooked, stir in cinnamon, nutmeg, honey, and almonds.

Serves 1

Cold Peach Porridge

¼ cup old fashioned oatmeal

2 oz. plain Greek yogurt

1 cup unsweetened almond milk

½ tsp chia seeds

¼ cup fresh peaches (chopped or sliced)

¼ tsp pure maple syrup

Mix oats, yogurt, milk and chia seeds together into a glass canning jar.

Place in fridge.

Let sit overnight.

Next day, add peaches and syrup.

TIP: Feel free to switch out the peaches with your favorite fruit.

Serves 1

Overnight Oats

1/3 cup old fashioned oats

1 scoop protein powder

¼ cup non-fat vanilla Greek yogurt

1/3 cup unsweetened vanilla almond milk

1 tsp honey

1/8 cup blueberries

½ of small banana sliced)

Cinnamon and nutmeg to taste

Mix all but fruit in a mason jar.

Then ad fruit and stir.

Place in refrigerator and enjoy the next morning.

Serves 1

Options: Make the base
of the overnight oat and
exclude the fruit. In
morning you can add
whatever fruit you
like...bananas,
strawberries, raisins,
etc. just stick to the
serving size listed above
for fruit.

Mushroom Omelet

½ cup egg whites

1 whole egg

1/8 cup onions

1/8 cup mushrooms

¼ cup cheddar cheese

Spray pan with cooking spray.

Add onion and mushrooms, sauté until almost cooked.

In separate bowl, mix egg and egg whites together.

Add egg to pan.

When egg firms, flip over to cook the other side.

Add cheese.

Fold egg over to melt the cheese.

Serves 1

Breakfast Pizza

3 cups of egg whites

6 whole eggs

2/3 cup bacon (cooked and chopped)

1 premade pizza crust

2/3 cup cheddar cheese

Preheat oven to 425 F

In bowl, whisk the eggs together.

Pour eggs into a sprayed pan, scramble until eggs are cooked.

Place pizza crust on pizza pan and add eggs and bacon.

Top with cheese.
Bake for 8-10 minutes.

Serves 6.

Serving size is one slice.

Canadian Western Omelet

½ cup egg whites

3 slices of Canadian bacon (chopped)

¼ cup mushrooms (cooked and chopped)

¼ cup green and red peppers (chopped)

1/8 cup cheddar cheese (shredded)

Mix eggs, mushroom, and bacon together.

Cook in sprayed pan.

Once eggs set, flip over egg.

Add cheese.

Serves 1

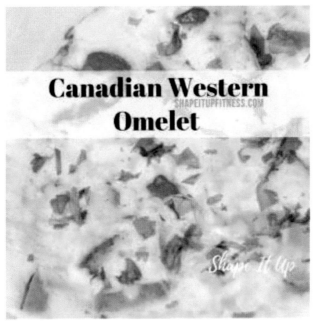

French Toast

2 slices of Ezekiel bread

2 egg whites

¼ cup unsweetened almond milk

1 tsp vanilla extract

Cinnamon to taste

Mix eggs, milk and vanilla extract in shallow square or rectangular container.

Dip bread into egg mixture.

Flip bread to coat both sides.

Spray medium pan with butter flavored cooking spray.

Once pan is hot, place egg-coated bread in pan.

Sprinkle top side of bread with cinnamon.

When bottom of bread is light golden brown, flip bread to cook the other side.

Sprinkle other side with cinnamon to taste.

Optional: 1/8 cup of pure maple syrup

Serves 1

Banana Pancakes

4 egg whites

1/3 cup rice flour

¾ cup yams

1 medium banana (mashed)

1 Tbsp walnuts (chopped)

Mix all ingredient together in bowl.

Spray small pan with butter flavored cooking spray.

Heat pan on medium heat.

Once pan is hot, pour mix into pan making small circles.

The pancakes will start to firm up and then flip to cook other side.

Optional: Top with 1/8 cup of pure maple syrup

Serves 1

TIP: I like to use a small pan and cook one pancake at a time because if you use a large pan the pancakes run into each other. Worth the extra time.

Strawberry Pancake

½ cup egg whites

½ cup dry old-fashioned oats

½ cup strawberries (chopped)

1 ½ Tbsp strawberry fruit spread

Mix all ingredients together in a medium bowl.

Spray pan with butter flavored spray.

Heat pan to medium heat.

Once pan is hot, pour mix into pan.

Let firm up then flip the pancake.

Optional: Top with 1/8 cup of pure maple syrup.

Serves 1

Strawberry Pineapple Pancakes

2 cup pancake mix

1 cup strawberries (chopped)

1 cup pineapple (chopped)

¼ cup pecans (chopped)

2 scoops of protein powder

Make pancakes according to mix directions.

Add strawberries, pineapple and pecans to pancake mix.

Cook pancakes according to packaging directions.

TIP: I like to use the large griddles to make a batch of pancakes. Spray griddle with butter flavored cooking spray. Heat on medium-high heat. Adjust temperature as needed. Use ¼ cup to pour out the pancake mix onto griddle.

Optional: Top with 1/8 cup of pure maple syrup.

1 serving is 2 pancakes

Pumpkin Pancake

½ cup egg whites

½ cup dry old-fashioned oats

½ cup pure pumpkin (not pumpkin pie mix)

Mix all ingredients together in a blender.

Using griddle (like in the Strawberry Pineapple Pancakes directions).

Optional: Top with 1/8 cup of pure maple syrup.

Serves 1

Yam Cakes

4 egg whites

½ cup old-fashioned dry oats

3 Tbsp pancake mix

¾ cup unsweetened almond milk

1 cup yam

Cinnamon to taste

Mix all ingredients together in blender.

Use the griddle instructions for pancakes.

Optional: Top with 1/8 cup pure maple syrup

Serves 2

MAIN DISHES

Mustard Shrimp

4 oz shrimp

3 oz Portabella mushrooms (chopped or sliced)

1 cup cooked green beans

1 cup cooked spaghetti squash

1 tsp stone ground mustard

Spray pan with butter flavored cooking spray.

Cook shrimp over medium heat until pink.

Once cooked, remove from pan and keep warm.

Add mushrooms to pan and sauté.

Right before mushrooms are cooked add squash and green beans to reheat.

Finally, add shrimp to warm up if needed.

Stir in mustard.

Serves 1

Shrimp Alfredo

3 oz cooked shrimp

4 oz cooked spaghetti squash

1 cup cooked broccoli

½ cup light cream cheese

1/8 cup unsweetened plain almond milk

1 tsp grated parmesan cheese

Garlic powder, onion powder and basil to taste.

Heat a medium pot on medium heat.

Add cream cheese, milk, parmesan and spices to pot.

Whisk ingredients until thick and smooth.

Add squash, shrimp and broccoli.

Stir until heated through.

Serves 1

Turkey Panini

2 slices of whole grain bread

3 oz deli turkey

2 slices turkey bacon

2 slices tomato

1 tsp Dijon mustard

½ apple (chopped)

1/8 Colby jack cheese

Heat panini grill to medium-high heat.

Lightly spray one side of bread with olive oil spray.

Place spray sides down on wax paper.

In small bowl, mix tomato, mustard, apple and cheese.

Spread mix onto dry side of bread slices.

Top break with turkey and bacon.

Put the bread together and make a sandwich (sprayed sides out).

Place on panini grill.

Grill until golden brown.

Serves 1

Tuna Sandwich

1 can tuna (in water and drained)

1 tsp thousand island dressing

1 Tbsp carrots (shredded and chopped)

1 celery stalk (raw and chopped)

1 leaf of romaine lettuce

2 slices of whole grain bread

Place tune in small bowl.

Add carrot, celery and depressing.

Add to tuna and mix.

Spread on bread.

Make sandwich.

Serves 1

Roasted Lunch

3 oz chicken (cooked and cubed)

½ cup cauliflower (raw)

½ cup sweet potato (cubed)

½ cup apple (large slices)

Salt and pepper to taste

Preheat oven 450 F

Spray cooking spray on baking sheets.

Place ingredients on pan.

Sprinkle salt and pepper.

Bake for 15- 20 minutes or until chicken is reheated.

Stir ½ way through baking time.

Serves 1

Ginger Pineapple Stir Fry

1 lb. pork tenderloin (cubed)

1 cup pineapple (chunks)

2 large carrots (chopped)

1 Tbsp ginger paste

½ tsp ground ginger

¼ cup sweet peas (frozen)

2 Tbsp coconut aminos

2 Tbsp soy sauce (reduced sodium)

1 cup white rice (cooked)

Spray pan with non-stick cooking spray.

Heat pan on medium-high.

Add tenderloin and sauté until no longer pink.

Remove and keep warm.

In same pan, add ginger paste, carrots, pineapple, peas, ground ginger, coconut aminos and soy sauce.

Stir until cooked (you can add little nit of pineapple juice if it starts to stick).

Add tenderloin back in to reheat.

Plate with rice and top with pork mix.

Serves 4

Crispy BBQ Chicken

1 lb. chicken tenderloins (raw)

3 oz crispy rice cereal (without BHT)

3 egg whites

Salt and pepper to taste

1 cup BBQ sauce

Preheat oven to 425 F

Using doble broil pan, spray pans with no-stick cooking spray.

Place cereal in plastic bag and crush.

Add slat and pepper to bag and shake.

In small bowl, beat egg whites.

Dip each chicken into cereal bag.

Shake until coated.

DO this for all the piece s of chicken.

Bake for 18-20 minutes until chicken is cooked.

Dip chicken into BBQ sauce.

Serves 4

Bruschetta

8 oz clams (drained and diced)

¼ cup grated parmesan and Reggiano cheese

¼ cup plum tomato (chopped)

½ cup spinach (chopped – fresh or frozen)

1 tsp garlic powder

1 tsp oregano

1 loaf French baguette

Heat over to 300F

Slice loaf of bread into 24 slices (about 10 grams per slice)

Place bread slices in oven on baking sheet.

Bale for 5-10 minutes or until crisp.

Mix all the rest of the ingredients together.

When bread is crispy, take out of oven and evenly spread tomato mix on each bread slice.

Increase oven temperature to 400F

Place back in the oven to bake an additional 5 minutes.

One serving equals 3 slices

Stuffed Tomato

4 tomato, large and firm

2 cups chicken breast (cut how you like it)

¼ cup avocado (mashed)

1 Tbsp onions (chopped)

Garlic powder and pepper to taste

2 Tbsp low-fat cream cheese

Old Bay seasoning to taste

Heat oven to 350 F

Wash and cut off tops of tomato.

Remove seeds and pulp.

Throw away seeds.

Chop up pulp for recipe.

Rinse out tomato and turn it upside down to drain.

Mix rest of ingredients (except Old Bay) in a bowl.

Spoon mixture into tomato.

Top with Old Bay.

Bake in oven for 10-15 minutes.

Serves 1

Ranch Chicken Pocket

3 oz chicken breast (cooked)

1 small tomato (chopped)

1 pita pocket

1 Tbsp low fat ranch dressing

Place chicken and tomato in small bowl.

 Mix in the ranch dressing.

Stuff chicken mix into pita.

Serves 1

Tuna Melts

1 Ezekiel (or whole grain) English muffin

1 can of water-based tuna

¼ cup artichoke hearts (drained, rinsed and chopped)

1 Tbsp light mayonnaise

1/8 cup Mexican blend cheese

Squeeze of lemon

Sprinkle of Old Bay seasoning

Set oven to broil.

Mix tuna, artichoke, mayo and lemon together in bowl.

Spray oven pan.

Place English muffin on pan.

Top English muffin with tuna mix.

Top with cheese and sprinkle Old Bay seasoning.

Place in over and cook for about 4-5 minutes or until cheese is melted.

Serves 1

Chinese Shrimp

3 oz cooked shrimp

1 cup cooked broccoli

1 Tbsp lite soy sauce or coconut aminos

½ cup cooked yam

Stir fry shrimp, broccoli and soy sauce in pan until hot.

Reheat yam in the microwave for 90 seconds on 70% power.

Serve yam on the side or mix it all together.

Serves 1

Ginger Shrimp

4 oz shrimp (cooked)

Ground ginger to taste

1 cup broccoli (cooked)

1 tsp ginger paste

1 tsp coconut aminos

½ Tbsp soy sauce (low sodium)

Sauté shrimp in sprayed pan over medium heat.

Sprinkle ginger on tope of shrimp as cooking.

Add little bit of water if shrimp sticks to pan.

Keep stirring.

Add broccoli to shrimp.

Add ginger paste, coconut amino and soy sauce and stir until coated.

Serves 1

Enchiladas

6 flour tortillas

1 lb. ground chicken (cooked)

1 cup salsa

2 oz cream cheese (low fat and softened)

½ cup Mexican cheese blend (shredded)

Taco spices to taste

Heat oven 350 F

Spray 13x9 pan.

Mix cream cheese, ¼ cup of Mexican cheese and tacos spices together.

Add chicken to cheese mix.

Stir until well combined.

Lay out tortillas.

Spoon mix on one side of tortilla.
Roll up each tortilla and place in pan.

Top with salsa and remaining Mexican cheese.
Cover with foil.

Bake for 2-25 minutes.

Serves 6

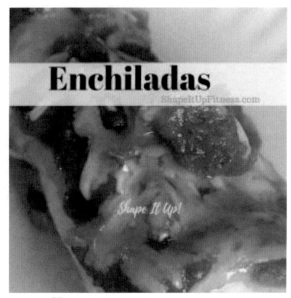

Thanksgiving Loaf

4 slices of whole grain bread

6 oz chicken broth (low sodium, fat free)

1.4 cup celery (chopped)

¼ cup egg whites

2 Tbsp poultry seasoning (1 Tbsp for bread, 1 Tbsp for turkey)

½ tsp rosemary

2 lbs. ground turkey

1/8 cup cranberry sauce (jellied)

Heat oven to 350 F

Chop up bread into cubes.

Pour broth into medium size saucepan.
Add bread and 1 Tbsp poultry seasoning and rosemary to pan.

Cover with lid and heat on medium-low until the bread becomes soft.

Stirring occasionally so it doesn't stick.

In large bowl, pour in egg white and 1 Tbsp poultry spices.

Mix with a whisk.

Add raw turkey to large bowl and mix together.
Add bread mixture to large bowl and mix well.

Add cranberries and mix well.

Place mix into sprayed loaf pan.

Bake at 350 F for 50-55 minutes

Then cover with foil and increase oven to 400 F cooking an additional 15 minutes.

Make sure it is cooked to internal temperature of 160 F.

Top each serving with 2 tsp of graving.

Serves 6

Thanksgiving Loaf

ShapeItUpFitness.com

Shape It Up!

Waldorf Salad

4 oz chicken (cooked and chopped)

¼ cup celery (chopped)

1 Tbsp light mayonnaise

1 tsp lemon juice

½ cup apple (chopped)

¼ cup grapes

1 tsp walnuts (chopped)

2 cups romaine lettuce

Mix all together.

Serves 1

Spinach Salad

4 cups spinach (raw)

1 whole hardboiled egg

1 hardboiled egg white

Red onions (sliced and to your taste)

4 slices or turkey bacon OR 2 slices regular bacon (cooked)

Assemble salad ingredients.

Dressing:

2 Tbsp stone ground mustard

¼ cup apple cider vinegar

Salt and pepper to taste

Whisk together and top on salad.

Serves 1

Chicken Spinach Sandwich

3-4 oz chicken tenderloin (cooked)

3 cups spinach (raw)

2 tsp mayonnaise

1 tsp grated parmesan cheese

1 potato roll

Place chicken and spinach in a sprayed pan.

Turn heat to medium and cover with lid.

Stir occasionally.

Spinach is done when it is reduced down.

Sprinkle cheese on chicken and spinach.

Place on roll with mayonnaise.

Serves 1

Open Faced Chicken

½ cup broccoli slaw

1 Tbsp mayonnaise (light)

2-3 oz chicken (cooked0

Salt and pepper to taste

1 slice of whole grain bread

Mix mayo, slaw, salt and pepper in small bowl.

Toast bread in toaster.

Top toast with chicken and slaw.

Serves 1

Marinara Burger

1 turkey burger patty

1 burger bun

1/8 cup marinara sauce

1 tsp shredded parmesan and Romano cheese

Burger spices to taste (oregano, black pepper, mesquite, etc.)

Cook turkey burger according to direction on package.

Sprinkle burger spices on top.

In small ramekin, heat up marinara sauce In microwave (30 seconds on 50% power or until warm).

Plate burger bun and add burger.

Sprinkle cheese on burger and then pour sauce on top.

Complete bun on top of burger.

Serves 1

Jerk Chicken

3 oz of chicken breast

½ cup broccoli slaw

Coleslaw Dressing (see below)

Jerk spices to taste

7-10 blue corn chips (about 30 grams)

Coleslaw Dressing:

2 Tbsp light mayonnaise

1 tsp cider vinegar

½ tsp Dijon mustard

½ tsp sugar

Combine coleslaw dressing ingredients in a small bowl. When chicken is done, plate chicken with slaw chips.

Serves 1

TIP: Crockpot Chicken – if you are power cooking chicken, you can cover chicken with jerk spices and cook in crockpot. Cook raw chicken breast for 6-8 hours on low or 4-6 hours on high (*crockpot times will vary).

Nachos

30 grams (about 7-10 chips depending on size) blue corn tortilla chips (look for brand with less than 5 ingredients)

½ cup ground chicken (cooked)

Taco spices to taste

1/8 cup sharp cheddar cheese

1/8 cup low fat sour cream

1/8 cup avocado

Heat oven to 350 F

Spray over pan with cooking spray.

Layer chips then top with chicken and cheese.

Cook for about 4-5 minutes or until cheese is melted.

Plate and top with sour cream and avocado.

Serves 1

Crab Wrap

1 cup imitation crab

1/8 cup raw celery (chopped)

½ Tbsp mayonnaise

Salt and pepper to taste

4-6 long leaves of romaine lettuce

4 oz sweet potato French fries

Combine crab, celery, mayonnaise, salt and pepper together in a bowl.

Wrap mix in lettuce leaves.

Cook sweet potato fries according to package.

Serve fries on the side.

Serves 1

BBQ Pizza

12-inch prepared pizza crust

¼ cup BBQ sauce (low sugar)

2 cups pork (cooked and shredded) *

2 oz Monterey jack cheese

***Pork cooked ahead of time**

Place 2 lbs. boneless pork butt in croc-pot.

Rub with salt and pepper.

Cook on low 6-8 hours or on high for 4-6 hours. Always make sure your meat is cooked using a meat thermometer.

Prepare oven based on pizza crust instructions.

Top pizza with all the above ingredients.

Bake for about 7-10 minutes

Serves 8

Tuna Casserole

6 oz egg noodles (cooked)

1 cup ricotta cheese, fat free

¾ cup fat -free plain Greek yogurt

½ cup flour

2 tsp Worcestershire sauce

Pepper to taste

½ cup peas (frozen)

8 oz mushrooms (chopped and cooked)

16 oz tuna fish (canned in water and drained)

1 cup Mexican low-fat cheese

Heat oven to 350 F

Mix ricotta, yogurt, flour, Worcestershire and pepper together in a large bowl.

Stir in tuna, peas, mushrooms until well combined.

Fold in cooked egg noodles.

Pour into a 13x9 baking dish.

Top with cheese.

Bake in oven for 25-30 minutes (the last 5 minutes tent a piece of aluminum foil over the top so the edges do not burn.

Serves 6

Tuna Casserole

Apple Pork Tenderloin

1 lbs. pork tenderloin

4 apples, de-cored, peeled and chopped

16 oz broccoli

5 lb. bag of carrots (you will have leftover carrots- consider this a power cooking option)

Cinnamon

Pork:

Place pork in crock-pot and add 1/8 cup of water.

Cook on low for 8-10 hours or high 6-8 hours. Always check if pork is done by using a meat thermometer.

Carrots:

Set oven to 350 F.

Peel and chop carrots into chunks.

Place on sprayed baking pan.

Spray a little olive oil on carrots.

Sprinkle with salt and pepper.

Bake in over for 45-60 minutes or until done to your liking.

Broccoli:

Microwave or steam fresh broccoli on stove top.

Apples:

Chop and sauté in a large pan with cinnamon.

Add water if the apples start to stick.

Once everything is cooked. Serve on plate.

Above makes 4 servings

One serving is:

3-4 oz pork

½ cup apples

¼ cup broccoli

¼ cup carrots

Zucchini Lasagne

2 large zucchini

1 lbs. ground chicken

14 oz marinara

14 oz fat free ricotta

1 cup low fat mozzarella cheese (shredded)

¼ cup grated parmesan cheese

Oregano and basil to taste

Heat oven to 350 degrees F.

Slice zucchini long ways.

Cook chicken in sprayed pan.

Once chicken cooked, pour marinara in with chicken and stir until heated.

In glass 8x8 dish, pour about 2 oz of marinara/chicken on the bottom of the dish.

Lay about 4-5 slices of zucchini down.

Smear about 2 oz of ricotta on top of zucchini.

Sprinkle some mozzarella and parmesan cheese on top of ricotta.

Repeat with layer of marinara/chicken then zucchini, then cheeses.

Finish top with mozzarella.

Sprinkle spices on top.

Cover with foil.

Bake for 30-40 minutes on 350 F

Remove foil and bake for another 10 minutes.

Let stand 10 minutes then serve.

Serves 6

Zucchini Lasagne

SHAPEITUPFITNESS.COM

Shape It Up

Ginger Parm Shrimp

1 cup cooked egg noodles (cooked)

1 cup shrimp

Ginger powder to taste

2 tsp butter

¾ cup broccoli (cooked)

1 tsp parmesan cheese

Add shrimp to sprayed and medium -high heated pan.

Add ginger to shrimp.

Stir.

Cook until shrimp is pink.

Then add in broccoli, egg noodles, butter and cheese.

Stir until hot.

Serves 1

Sloppy Joe Chicken

2 cups chicken (cooked and shredded)

¼ cup ketchup

1 Tbsp Dijon mustard

1 Tbsp Worcestershire sauce

1 Tbsp tomato paste

1 tsp red wine vinegar

8 oz sodium-free tomato sauce

4 burger buns

In large sauce pot, mix all the ingredients from ketchup down to tomato sauce together.

Add chicken to the mix.

Heat on stove top on medium heat.

When heated, place chicken on bun.

Serves 4

Cheese Steak

1/8 cup onions (sliced)

¼ cup mushrooms (chopped)

2 oz sirloin steak (cut in strips)

Small hoagie roll (about 50 grams)

1/8 cup sharp cheddar cheese

1 Tbsp ketchup

Sauté onions and mushrooms in a sprayed hot pan.

Remove once cooked and keep warm.

Add steak to pan and cook until desired temperate.

Add onion and mushrooms back to pan.

Top with cheese and melt.

Plate roll and add steak then ketchup.

Serves 1

Seafood Bowtie Pasta

½ cup cooked bowtie pasta

3 oz raw shrimp

2 oz imitation crabmeat

1 tsp grated parmesan cheese

1 cup cooked broccoli

Cook pasta according to directions of package.

Once pasta is drained, set aside and keep warm.

In same pot the pasta was cooked in, spray olive oil in pot add the shrimp and cook until pink.

Add crabmeat and broccoli to pot.

Stir until cooked through.

Portion out pasta then top with seafood mixture.

Top with cheese.

Serves 1

Clams Pasta

1 cup of cooked pasta (your choice)

¼ cup spaghetti sauce

2 cans of clams (13 oz total) drained

To taste: Basil and oregano

1 tsp grated parmesan cheese

Mix all together and reheat either in microwave or on stove top.

Serves 1

Tip: Cook a full box (or 2) of pasta in one shot.

Tip: When reheating spaghetti sauce, put the sauce in a small bowl when reheating then add to meal after everything is hot. It tends to get watery when you heat the sauce with the food.

Salmon Feta Pasta

4 oz smoked salmon

½ cup bowtie pasta

1 cup spinach

1 Tbsp feta (low-fat)

Salt and pepper to taste

Cook pasta according to package directions.

Once pasta is drained, set aside and keep warm.

In same pot, spray olive oil and add salmon and spinach.

Warm until spinach wilts.

Portion out the pasta.

Top with salmon, spinach and cheese.

Tip: You can also keep the salmon cold if you like. Just top at the end. This recipe is also good with asparagus.

Serves 1

Eggplant Pizza

1 eggplant (about 2 ½ pounds)

2 egg whites

2 oz cooked ground turkey

½ cup panko breadcrumbs

Spaghetti spices (garlic powder, oregano, basil, onion powder, etc.) to taste

½ cup marinara sauce

½ cup mozzarella cheese

Clean and slice eggplant in ¼ inch thick circles.

Pour egg whites into container.

In separate container, pour in panko and spices then mix.

Coat both sides of the eggplant in the egg then dredge eggplant in the panko mixture coating both sides.

Add breaded eggplant to hot pan that has been sprayed with cooking spray. Once bottom is golden brown, flip to cook other side.

Warm marinara and turkey in the microwave oven for 1-2 minutes at 70% power

With eggplant still in pan, top each eggplant circle with warm marinara with turkey.

Add cheese on top of each eggplant.

Place lid on the pan to melt the cheese.

Serves 2

Chicken Pizza

4oz chicken

1 cup spinach

1 small Roma tomato

¼ cup mozzarella cheese

1 flatbread

Heat oven to 400 degrees F.

Place flatbread on sprayed cookie sheet.

Add toppings.

Cook for about 4-5 minutes.

Serves 1

Margaretta Pizza

1 cup spinach (raw)

1 small Roma tomato

1/8 cup mozzarella cheese

1 flatbread

Heat over to 400 degrees F.

Place ingredients on flatbread.

Place in oven and cook for about 4-5 minutes.

TIP: I like my flatbread lightly baked so if you like a crunchier crust cook a little longer.

Serves 1

Salsa Chicken Two Ways

4 oz chicken (cooked and reheated)

½ cup potato (cooked and reheated)

4 Tbsp salsa

1 Tbsp sour cream

Two Options:

1. Place salsa on chicken. Sour cream on potato.

2. Layer potato, chicken, salsa and then sour cream.

Serves 1

Chicken Mash Up

3 oz ground chicken (cooked)

½ cup mashed sweet potatoes (cooked)

1 cup cauliflower (cooked)

Combine all in a bowl and reheat in microwave or on stove top.

Serves 1

Fish Tacos

3-4 oz tilapia

½ lemon (fresh squeezed lemon juice)

½ cup coleslaw mix (plain no dressing)

2 tsp tartar sauce

Salt and pepper to takes

1 small flour tortillas

Mix coleslaw, tartar, salt and pepper in a large bowl.

Spray cooking oil into pan.

On medium heat cook tilapia in lemon juice.

Fish should flake when it is done.

Place fish on tortilla

Top with coleslaw mix.

Serves 1

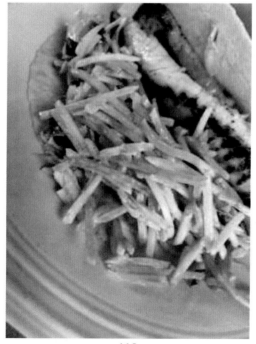

Scallops Butter Linguine

½ cup cooked linguine

½ cup scallops

2 tsp butter

½ cup spaghetti squash (cooked)

½ cup spinach (raw)

1 tsp grated parmesan cheese

Basil to taste

In pan, spray with cooking oil and butter.

Add scallops and cook until lightly brown on one side.

Flip over scallop to brown other side.

Add spinach and squash around scallops.

Place linguine on top of spinach.

Place lid on pan.

Once spinach is wilted and linguine is heated, plate then top with cheese and basil.

Serves 1

Grilled Pork with Sweet Potato

Spices:

1 Tbsp basil

1 Tbsp thyme

1 tsp black pepper

1 tsp rosemary

1 tsp paprika

Sea salt to taste

1 lbs. pork tenderloin (cut into 12 pieces)

Sweet Mashed Potatoes (recipe)

1 cup broccoli (cooked)

Mix spices in small bowl.

Rub spices on pork slices.

Heat grill (I like the little indoor grills) and spray with cooking spray.

Add pork to grill.

Cook until no longer pink in center.

Plate and serve with broccoli and Sweet Mashed Potatoes.

Serves 4

A1 Chicken

4oz chicken (cooked)

1 cup broccoli (cooked)

½ cup yam (cooked)

1 Tbsp A1 sauce

Reheat all together.

Serves 1

Beef Stroganoff

1 package of egg noodles

1 lbs. boneless sirloin streak (cut into strips)

2 cups portabella mushrooms

½ tsp onion powder

½ cup non-fat plain Greek yogurt

½ cup low fat sour cream

1 Tbsp flour

2 tsp Dijon mustard

¼ tsp salt

1/8 tsp white pepper

Cook pasta according to directions.

Set aside and keep warm.

In small bowl, made sauce mix from onion powder down list to white pepper.

In sprayed pan heated to med-high, add steak and mushrooms.

Cook until lightly browned.

Reduce heat and add sauce mix to pan.

Stir until
thickens.

Plate with pasta.

Serves 6

Plain and Simple

4oz chicken (cooked)

1 cup green beans

¾ cup yams (cooked)

Place on plate and reheat in microwave for 2-3 minutes on 70% power.

OR

Reheat on stove in small pot.

Serves 1

Mexican Chicken

4 oz chicken (cooked)

¾ cup potato (cooked)

4 Tbsp salsa

1 Tbsp sour cream

Combine chicken, potato and salsa on a plate.

Reheat in microwave 2-3 minutes on 70% power or on stove.

Once warm, add sour cream.

Serves 1

Chicken Chipotle

4 oz chicken (chopped)

1 cup spinach

1 small Roma tomato (chopped)

1 Tbsp chipotle dressing

Spray pan with cooking spray.

Heat pan on medium heat.

Place chicken in hot pan.

Cook until chicken is almost done (no pink inside).

Add spinach and tomato.

Cook until chicken and veggies are done to your taste.

Add chipotle dressing and stir.

Serves 1

Chicken and Broccoli

All precooked:

4 oz chicken

1 cup broccoli

½ cup yam

Place on plate and reheat.

Serves 1

Mustard Chicken

4 oz chicken (cooked)

1 tsp stone ground mustard

5 oz portabella mushrooms

¼ cup chicken broth (99% fate free and low sodium)

½ cup potato (cooked)

1 cup green bean (cooked)

Whisk mustard and broth in small bowl until combined.

Reheat chicken, green beans and potatoes.

Top with mustard mix.

Serves 1

Tarragon Chicken

3 oz chicken (cooked)

1 cup green beans

3 oz portabella mushrooms

¼ cup chicken broth (99% fat free and low sodium)

½ cup potato (cubed and cooked)

1 ½ Tbsp Dijon mustard

1 tsp tarragon

Spray pan with non-stick spray.

Place pan on stove and heat at medium.

Add potatoes and chicken to pan.

If at any time food starts to stick just add a little bit of water to pan and put lid on until you get some steam. Then stir.

Add green beans and mushrooms.

In separate bowl, mix broth, mustard and tarragon together.

Pour broth mixture into a pan and quickly lid.

Cook for about 1 minute more on low heat until sauce thickens.

Serves 1

Turkey Taco

2 corn taco shells

4 oz ground turkey (cooked)

1 Tbsp picante or salsa

1 cup romaine lettuce (shredded)

Taco seasoning to taste

Heat ground turkey, picante sauce and taco seasoning in the microwave 1-2 minutes on 60% power or on stove top.

Add turkey mixture to corn shell.

Top with romaine.

Serves 1

Meatballs

1 lbs. ground turkey

¼ cup panko breadcrumbs

1 whole egg

Italian spices (garlic powder, onion powder, basil, oregano) to taste.

Combine above ingredients until well mixed.

Form mix into meatball shapes.

Place on sprayed, hot pan.

Cook until there is no pink in the center.

Serves 4

To Make It Into A Meal

1 cup zucchini (cut how you like)

¼ cup marinara sauce

1 tsp grated parmesan cheese

Spray pan and sauté zucchini in pan.

When cooked, drain any water from zucchini.

Add marinara to pan with zucchini.

Heat until sauce is hot.

Pour onto plate.

Top with meatballs and parmesan cheese.

Serves 1

"Chilly "Stew

1 lbs. ground turkey (cooked)

2 ½ cups tomatoes (diced)

½ cup salsa

1 can black beans

½ cup sweet corn

½ cup onion

½ green pepper

2 cloves of garlic

1 oz tortilla corn chips

In a large pot, spray the bottom of pot with cooking spray.

Heat on medium-high.

Place onions, garlic and peppers in pot.

Sauté until tender.

Add the rest of the ingredients except the chips.

Stir.

Lower heat to low.

Simmer until the stew thickens up.

Stir occasionally.

Pour into a bowl with chips on the side.

Makes 8 servings

Sneaky Burgers

1 lbs. ground turkey

½ cup onions

½ cup spinach (frozen or cooked)

½ cup tomatoes

Couple of dashes of Worcestershire sauce

4 egg whites

Spices to taste – Sea salt, garlic powder, mesquite

Mix Worcestershire, eggs and spices in small bowl.

In another bowl, mix turkey, onions, spinach and tomatoes.

Add wet mix to dry mix.

Blend well with hands.

Form into patties.

Can be cooked then or can be frozen raw for later OR cook then freeze.

Makes 4 burgers

For a meal:

1 burger

2 slices of whole grain bread/bun

½ of an avocado.

Prepare burger and top with avocado and bread.

Serves 1

Parmesan "Spaghetti"

1 cup squash and or zucchini (cooked)

3 oz ground turkey (cooked)

2 oz portabella mushrooms (cooked)

1 tsp grated parmesan cheese

Reheat all the ingredients in a pot on the stove or in microwave 2-3 minutes on 70% power or until heated.

Serves 1

Squashed Spaghetti

4 oz ground turkey (cooked)

¼ cup spinach

1 cup zucchini (chopped)

1 cup spaghetti squash (cooked)

¼ cup marinara sauce

1 tsp grated parmesan cheese

Place all but marinara and cheese in a pot to reheat.

Once warm, add marinara and cheese.

Serves 1

Steak N' Egg Omelet

4 egg whites

2 oz steak (cooked)

1 cup broccoli (cooked)

1/8 cup white sharp cheddar cheese

Cook eggs in sprayed pan.

Add steak and broccoli to reheat.

Fold steak, broccoli and cheese into egg.

Cover with lid until cheese is melted.

Serves 1

Beef Avocado

2 oz steak (chopped)

2 oz portabella mushrooms (chopped)

¼ of an avocado

½ oz cheddar cheese

1 oz tortilla chips

2 cups romaine lettuce (chopped)

Sauté steak and mushrooms in pan.

Cook until steak is to desired tenderness.

Layer on a plate the chips, lettuce, steak, cheese and avocado.

Serves 1

BBQ Chicken

3-4 oz chicken breast (cooked)

2 Tbsp low/no sugar BBQ sauce

2/3 cup green beans (cooked)

Small roll (about 40-50 grams)

2 tsp butter

Reheat chicken, green beans and BBQ sauce in microwave or on stove top.
Serve with roll and butter.

Serves 1

TIP: When microwaving, put BBQ sauce in small separate bowl.

SNACKS AND SIDES

Deviled Eggs

3 hard-boiled eggs (de-shelled)

½ Tbsp mayonnaise

1 tsp stone ground mustard

Pepper to taste

See instructions on how to hard-boil eggs.

Cut a long-wise slit in each egg (trying not to cut the yolk).

Open eggs and pop out the yolk.

Put one yolk in a small bowl and discard (or save for something else) other two yolks.

Mash one yolk with a fork.

Add mayonnaise, mustard and pepper to yolk.

Mix together until creamy.

Spread yolk mixture between the 3 eggs (you will have 6 halves).

Add paprika or parsley for garnish if you like.

Serves 1

Homemade Tortilla Chips

1 small or medium tortilla wrap

Olive oil spray

Salt

Tip: Use other spices or seasonings you like. Examples could be taco seasoning, salt and pepper, Italian spices, cinnamon and nutmeg. Be creative.

Spray wrap lightly with olive oil.

Cut into triangles.

Spread out on a sprayed baking sheet.

Sprinkle salt and spices.

Bake at 350 degrees F for about 12-15 minutes (rotating baking sheet ½ way through).

Pair the chips with a protein and fat (like deli turkey rolled and avocado) or use in another meal.

Serves 1

Potato Chips

2 medium size baking potatoes

1 Tbsp olive oil

Salt and pepper to taste

TIP: Can use other spices like taco, parsley, chicken spices, etc. for different flavors.

Slice potatoes into sticks or coin shapes.

Pour olive oil into a bowl or plastic bag.

Toss potatoes into olive oil.

Add spices to potatoes.

Coat the potatoes in the oil and spices.

Spread on sprayed cooking sheet.

Bake at 375 degrees for 15-20 minutes.

Check on them often as oven temperature may vary and also depending on how thick or thin the slices of potatoes are.

4 oz is one serving

Fake Mashed "Potatoes"

1 large cauliflower (cut into tiny small pieces)

14 oz chicken broth (fat free and low sodium)

3 garlic cloves (chopped) can buy in jar pre-chopped

Parsley to taste

Combine cauliflower, broth and garlic in large pot.

If broth doesn't cover cauliflower, add water to just cover.

Bring to a boil on high heat.

Once boiling, reduce heat to medium-low and simmer for about 15 minutes or until cauliflower is tender.

Drain cauliflower and garlic, reserving 2 Tbsp of broth.

Use immersion blender to blend.

Add reserved broth to keep it moist.

Season with salt, pepper or any other spices you like.

1 cup is one serving

Sweet Mashed Potato

½ cup sweet potatoes (cooked and mashed)

Cinnamon to taste

1 tsp butter

Mix together and reheat.

Serves 1

TIP: Use the power cooking method for the sweet potatoes.

"Grab-N-Go" Snack Options

Air popped popcorn

Rice cakes (can add spices to plain)

TIP: Buy plain rice cakes. Crumble them up in a plastic bag. Add your favorite spices and give it a shake. Some spice options might be cinnamon, nutmeg, taco, salt and pepper, lemon pepper...be creative.

Nuts and fruit

Cheese sticks

Protein shakes

Hard-boiled egg whites

Nuts (about 5 whole pieces is one serving) including any unsalted almonds, peanuts, walnuts, etc.

Raw veggies and hummus

Protein bars (choose wisely, most are glorified candy bars)

Leave In Your Desk Or Car

Items that do not need refrigeration.

Proportioned nuts (whatever you like, no salt added is ideal) and banana

Protein powder and shaker cup along with "drink box" type of milk (almond, rice, etc.)

Pouches of tuna or salmon and crackers with mustard

TIP: if you live in an area that your car will turn into a heat inferno be mindful of what you leave in there. Food can spoil easily in the heat. When in doubt, throw it out.

DESSERTS

Apples Crescents

2 large apples (chopped)

1 can refrigerated biscuit crescents (organic if possible)

½ Tbsp walnut (chopped)

Cinnamon

Place apples and walnut in a small bowl.

Sprinkle cinnamon (to taste) over apples and walnuts.

Unroll biscuits into individual triangles.

Fill each biscuit with apple mix.

Fold the biscuit around the apple mix. No holes showing.

Bake according to biscuit directions.

Optional: top each dough ball with 1 tsp real whipped cream

Makes 5   servings

Brownie In A Cup

1 whole egg

1 scoop of chocolate protein powder

1 Tbsp natural peanut butter

1 Tbsp water

Mix ingredients in a coffee mug.

Cook in microwave for 1 minute on HIGH.

If additional time is needed for it to set, heat for additional 30 seconds on HIGH until done.

Serves 1

Quick Banana Muffins

3 large bananas (ripe)

½ cup sugar

1 egg

1 ½ cup flour

1 tsp baking powder

1/3 cup unsweetened applesauce

Preheat oven to 350 F

Prepare muffin tin with cupcake liners.

Mash banana with fork in medium size bowl.

Lightly beat egg in separate small bowl.

Pour egg in with bananas.

Add sugar.

Mix together.

Stir in applesauce.

In separate medium bowl, mix flour and baking powder.

Add dry ingredients to wet ingredients.

Mix.

Pour batter into muffin tins about 2/3 full.

Bake for 15-20 minutes or until toothpick comes out clean.

Serving size is one muffin.

Oatmeal Peach Cookies

1 cup instant oats

¾ cup flour

1 ½ tsp cinnamon

1 ½ tsp baking powder

¼ tsp salt

2 Tbsp unsweetened applesauce

1 egg

1 tsp vanilla extract

½ cup honey

½ cup peached (diced)

In medium bowl, mix oats, flour, cinnamon, salt and baking powder together.

In another bowl, whisk applesauce, egg, and vanilla extract.

Stir in honey.

Add flout mis to wet mix.

Stir until just incorporated.

Gently fold in peaches.

Place in refrigerator for 60 minutes.

Preheat over to 325 and line cookie sheet with parchment paper.

Drop 16 rounded cookies onto sheet.

Bake 12-15 minutes.

Cool on pan for 10 minutes.

Finish cooling on wire rack

Makes 16 cookies

One serving is one cookie.

Ricotta Parfait

¼ cup non-fat vanilla Greek yogurt

¼ cup ricotta (low or non-fat)

¼ cup strawberries

¼ cup banana

¼ cup blueberries

½ tsp almonds (sliced)

Mix all together.

Serves 1

Pineapple Strawberry Pudding Cake

1 box yellow cake mix

For cake mix – use in place of (substitutions):

    Eggs: 1 egg +2 egg whites

    Oil: ½ cup unsweetened applesauce

    Water: ½ cup pineapple juice from can +3/4 cup water

1 box instant vanilla pudding

1 cup pineapple

1 cup strawberries

Preheat over not 350 F.

Spray Bundt cake with floured spray.

In mixer, add cake mix (and substitutions) and pudding mix.

Mix until combined.

In separate bowl, add pineapple and strawberries and chop then up using double bladed kitchen scissors.

Stir in pineapple and strawberries into the cake mix.

Once combined, pour into prepared Bundt pan.

Bake for 45-60 minutes (ovens vary)

Cake is done when toothpick comes out clean.

    Cool in pan for about 10 minutes.
    Flip onto rack and cool completely.

Serves 16

Pineapple Strawberry
Pudding Cake

ShapeItUpFitness.com

Shape It Up!

Strawberry Waffles

1 toaster waffle

¼ cup vanilla ice cream

5-6 whole strawberries

Toast waffle according to package.

Top with ice cream and strawberries.

Serves 1

Carrot Cake Cookies

Cookie

Dry Ingredients

1 ½ cup flour

¾ cup oats (blended)

1 tsp ground cloves

1 tsp nutmeg

½ tsp pumpkin pie spices

½ tsp baking soda

Wet Ingredients

6 Tbsp butter (softened)

6 Tbsp unsweetened applesauce

¼ cup sugar

¼ cup light brown sugar

1 egg white

Rest of Ingredients

2 cups carrots (finely grated)

1/8 cup walnuts (chopped)

Preheat oven to 350 F

Line cookie sheet with parchment paper.

Whisk dry ingredients in a large bowl.

In mixer, combine wet ingredients.

Blend on med-high until light and fluffy (about 4-6 minutes)

Slowly add in dry ingredients to mixer until combined.

Fold in carrots.

Fold in walnuts.

Spoon 24 cookies of even shape onto parchment paper.

Bake for 20 minutes or until golden brown on bottom with center slightly soft.

Cool cookies on rack.

While cookies are cooling make filling (on next page)

After cookies are cooled, take 2 cookies and smear filling on one side and top with the other cookie.

Makes 12 complete cookies (24 cookies total = 12 sandwiches)

One serving is one complete cookie (2 cookies and filling).

Filling for Carrot Cake Cookies

8 oz marshmallow fluff

3 oz cream cheese (low-fat)

3 Tbsp butter (softened)

1 tsp vanilla extract

Using a hand mixer, blend ingredients until light and fluffy.

Raisin Nut Pumpkin Muffins

¼ cup brown sugar

1/8 cup coconut sugar

1/8 cu sugar

4 oz unsweetened applesauce

2 tsp cinnamon

1 ½ tsp ginger, ground

½ tsp cloves

1 tsp baking powder

1 tsp baking soda

½ tsp salt

2 Tbsp vanilla extract

4 egg whites

15 oz pumpkin (not pumpkin pie mix)

2 cups oat flour

2 scoops protein powder

½ cup unsweetened almond milk

1/3 cup walnuts (chopped)

½ cup raisins

Heat oven to 350 F

Line muffin tins with cupcake liners.

Combine sugars, applesauce, spices, baking powder, baking soda, extract and pumpkin in large bowl.

Mix well.

In separate bowl, mix the flour, protein powder and milk together.

The add the wet ingredients to the dry and mix until combined.

Pour about ¼ cup of batter into each muffin tin.

Bake for about 10-15 minutes or until a toothpick comes out clean of the center.

Makes about 16 muffins.

Serving size is 2 muffins.

Chocolate Chip Protein Cookies

2 cups old fashioned oats

¼ tsp salt

8 scoops of protein powder

1 tsp baking soda

3 Tbsp butter

9 Tbsp unsweetened applesauce

2 tsp vanilla extract

1 egg white

¼ cup sugar

¼ cup chocolate mini chips

Preheat oven to 350 F

Line pan with parchment paper.

Grind oats in blender until it looks like flour.

Add oats to a large bowl then mx in protein powder, salt an baking soda.

Cream butter and sugar in mixer.

Mix well.

Add egg, vanilla and mix.

Stir in chocolate chips.

Shape into balls and flatten out on parchment paper.

For larger cookies (8 per batch), bake for about 20-25 minutes (check on them every 5 minutes after the 10-minute mark). For smaller cookie, bake for 8-10 minutes or until edge start to get golden brown.

Cool for about 10-15 minutes on cookie rack.

DO NOT EAT THESE RIGHT AWAY!

Once cool, individually wrap each cookie in wax paper and place in container with lid. I know you will be tempted to eat right away but if you wait one day you will have a deliciously moist cookie!

TIP: They don't spread so they can be close to each other. I made these cookies fairly large.

Makes 8 cookies. Serving is one cookie.

These will last in container on counter for about 7 days.

Chocolate Chip Protein Cookies

Frozen Yogurt Bites

½ cup strawberries, frozen

½ Tbsp powdered sugar

1 cup vanilla non-fat Greek yogurt

Place frozen strawberries in microwave safe bowl.

Thaw in microwave for about 1 minute on 70% power. (you don't want to cook it so there should be a little bit of ice crystals on the strawberries).

Remove the strawberries and chop them with kitchen scissors.

Whisk the yogurt and sugar together in small bowl.

Stir in strawberries.

Using an ice cube try (I used Han Solo from Star Wars ice cube trays).

Pour the mixture into the tray and spread out evenly in each cube.

TIP: If using silicon ice cube tray, then put tray into a loaf pan to keep the tray stable transporting it into the freezer.

Place plastic wrap over the ice cube tray and freeze overnight.

After frozen, "crack" them off the ice cube tray and eat as a frozen treat.

Serves 1

Melted Nuggets

1 bar of all-natural chocolate chip cookie dough bar

Heat oven 250 F

Cut the bar into 6-8 pieces.

Place bar on small baking pan that is lined with parchment paper.

Heat in over until they are slightly mushy (about 3-5 minutes depending on thickness).

Pull out of oven.

Allow them to cook for about 3 minutes.

Peel them off parchment paper and eat.

Serves 1

Option: You can mush them flat to make them more like tiny cookies but don't make them too thin or they will burn).

Creamy Egg White

4 egg whites

¼ cup cream cheese (low fat)

Cinnamon to taste

Spray pan with butter spray.

Add eggs and cook on both sides.

Lay cream cheese down the center of the egg.

Sprinkle with cinnamon.

Fold over and let cream cheese soften.

Serves 1

Optional: Can add drizzle of pure maple syrup. Or place fruits in the inside of egg. Some suggestions are apples, bananas, mangos, pumpkin, etc.

Pineapple Squares

8 sheets of graham crackers

2 Tbsp sugar

½ cup sugar

¼ cup butter (melted)

¾ cup fat free vanilla Greek yogurt

½ cup light cream cheese (softened)

¼ cup orange marmalade

1 can (20 oz) crushed unsweetened pineapple, drain and reserve 4 oz juice

1 envelope of unflavored gelatin

Crumb base:

Mix graham cracker crumbs, 2 Tbsp of sugar and butter in 8x8 inch dish.

Press mix into bottom of dish.

Place in freezer for 10 minutes.

Filling:

Blend yogurt, cream cheese, ½ cup sugar and marmalade with hand mixer.

Gelatin mix:

Sprinkle gelatin over pineapple juice in small saucepan.

Let sit for 1 minute.

Cook on low heat while stirring until gelatin dissolves.

Beat gelatin mix into filling until well blended.

Pour evenly over crumb base.

In small bowl, stir together pineapple and rest of marmalade.

Evenly spoon over filling.

Cover with plastic wrap and refrigerate for about 2 hours or until firm.

Makes 16 servings

Blueberry Lemon Muffins

2 cups flour

4 tsp baking powder

½ tsp salt

¼ cup butter

¼ cup unsweetened applesauce

1 cup sugar

4 tsp lemon zest

1 whole egg

2 egg whites

½ cup buttermilk

1 ½ cup blueberries (fresh or frozen – thawed and drained)

Preheat over to 375 degrees F

Line muffin tins with cupcake liners.

In small bowl, sift flour and baking powder together.

In mixer, blend butter, sugar, eggs, salt, lemon and buttermilk.

Add flour mix to blender mix.

Blend until combined.

Fold in blueberries.

Fill muffin tins 2/3 full.

Bake for about 25-30 minutes or until toothpick comes out clean.

Makes 16 muffins.

Serving size is one muffin.

"Cannoli" Cake

1 slice (about 75 grams) of angel food cake (bought in grocery store)

¼ cup fat free ricotta

1 tsp granulated sugar

1 tsp vanilla extract

2 tsp mini chocolate chips

Mix ricotta, sugar and extract in small bowl.
Slice cake.

Top cake with ricotta mixture.

Sprinkle chips on top.

Serves 1

Chocolate Banana Angel Food Cake

1 slice (about 75 grams) of angel food cake (buy in bakery section of grocery store)

1 small (about 2/3 cup) banana (sliced)

¼ cup vanilla ice cream

1 tsp mini chocolate chips

Layer cake, banana, ice cream and then chips.

Serves 1

Strawberry Sundae

½ cup vanilla ice cream

¾ cup strawberries (frozen or fresh)

If using frozen strawberries, place strawberries in bowl.

Microwave for about 1 minute on power 70% or until they are mostly thawed.

Mash them in a bowl

Scoop out ice cream.

Pour strawberries over top of ice cream.

Serves 1

Peanut Butter Chocolate Chip Muffins

1 cup all-purpose flour

¼ tsp baking soda

1/8 tsp salt

¾ granulated sugar

¼ cup packed dark brown sugar

¼ cup creamy peanut butter

1 tsp vegetable oil

1 tsp vanilla extract

1 large egg

1 large egg white

¼ cup semisweet chocolate min chips

Preheat over to 350 degrees F.

Put muffin paper in muffin tin pan.

Combine flour, soda and salt in a bowl.

In a separate bowl, combine sugars and remaining ingredients (except chocolate chips).

Stir until well blended.

Add flour mixture to sugar mixture.

Stirring just until blended.

Add chocolate chips.

Fill muffin tins to about 2/3 full.

Bake at 350 F for about 15-20 minutes.

Cool on a wire rack

Serving size is 1 muffin.

Yields 16 servings

Protein Pudding

This requires prepping the night before.

1 box of vanilla cook-n-serve pudding

TIP: Instant pudding, although easier to make, typically had BHT in it so check your labels

Follow the instructions for the pudding.

TIP: If using almond milk use just a little less than if you were to use cow's milk.

Once cooked and cooled, pour pudding into individual cups and place in refrigerator.

When you are ready to eat them, add 1 scoop of protein powder and stir with a fork until the powder is mixed in.

Add a tsp of whipped cream.

TIP: Use flavored protein powders to change the flavor of the pudding or use different flavored pudding.

Make sure you add protein powder RIGHT before you eat the pudding.

Take serving size off the pudding box.

1 Serving will be pudding serving from box and 1 scoop protein powder.

Banana Puff

5 vanilla wafer cookies

5 tsp banana pudding (can use the protein pudding recipe)

5 tsp whipped cream

Lay out wafer cookies.

Place 1 tsp pudding on each cookie

Top with 1 tsp whipped cream per cookie.

Serves 1

ABOUT THE AUTHOR

NICOLE SIMONIN is an ACE Personal Trainer, ACE Health Coach, host of *"Shape It Up Over 40"* podcast, author of *"The No Fuss, No Mess Shape It Up Cookbook"*, founder of Shape It Up, LLC, licensed Physical Therapist Assistant and former professional ballet dancer. Nicole has been featured in Racheal Ray in Season, Bicycling Magazine, Real Simple and MSN to name a few. Since 2006, Nicole has been helping women lost weight for the last time. To learn more, go to ShapeItUpFitness.com

Grab Your BONUS Meal Plans!
ShapeItUpFitness.com/meals

Made in the USA
Middletown, DE
14 October 2020